PRA

"Easy to Use is an easy to read book that provides practical advice on topics that matter to UX teams - from maturity of UX organizations, integrating UX into agile, and organizing UX teams for success. I encourage UX leaders to tap into Sean's wealth of experience."

–Janaki Kumar
VP, Head of Design and Co-Innovation Center, America, SAP Labs

"This book is an excellent introduction and overview of User Experience design (UX) and how to fit it into an agile development methodology. I recommend this book to anyone wanting to better understand what it is and how to integrate it into an agile software development methodology."

–Chris Claborne
Enterprise Architect, Office of the CIO, Qualcomm

"It's refreshing to see the thoughtfulness and design expertise Sean Van Tyne brings to the enterprise software space. It is a technology category that's ripe for design-led disruption, and this book will help you get there. From agile software development to UX maturity models, Easy to Use 2.0 is packed full of useful and actionable information. Better yet, there's something in here for everyone; there are business insights for the design leader and design insights for the business leader."

–Garron Engstrom
Product Design at Facebook

"Most user experience literature today focuses on consumer experiences but what if your customer and your end-user are different people? In B2B situations, that's exactly the case. In Easy to Use, Sean Van Tyne takes on the complex topic of agile software development for enterprise software and unleashes his expertise in user experience and design thinking. The result is an easy to understand, easy to implement, and easy to use guide to creating simple yet effective enterprise applications."

–Steve Craig
Products & Experience Director, Mitek

"A great primer on how Experience Design can transform your Enterprise Software with specifics on how to implement it in your organization. Sean Van Tyne manages to be both comprehensive and concise, providing case studies, samples, and applies experience design wisdom across all phases of the product life cycle."

–Jonathan Wagner
Interaction Designer, Usability Engineer, and Design Project Manager, Hewlett Packard

"The intersection of the customer, user and technology is at the heart of this concise guidebook for developing easy to use software. That's exactly where it should be! In Easy to Use Sean Van Tyne shares essential insights from his successful career determining, developing and deploying extraordinary user experiences at many of the best companies. Doing software development effectively with design thinking while leveraging Agile development processes is not an option. You want Easy to Use as your software development companion. Particularly where business wins, losses and profits depend on user experience being different and better than the competition."

"Enterprise UX is screaming for this book! It helps product teams orient themselves to where they are in the UX continuum, how to effectively plan while still syncing with Agile's short iterations and, most importantly, how what we do is more about people than technology. Anyone serious about improving enterprise UX will find this cradle to grave manual indispensable!"

"Regardless of whether you're just starting to get serious about UX or you're figuring out the best way to organize existing UX efforts, this book strips out verbose philosophy and gets to the point. Gauge where your group is at on the UX continuum, how to easily measure effectiveness, which deliverables to use for different scenarios and why, and important tips for integrating with Agile. Great book!"

"This book is for anyone responsible for User Experience in your organization; from designers to product owners, developers and more. What Sean describes is an exact recipe for success that is rigorous yet easy to understand and take immediate action on. Easy to Use has something for everyone in an organization... leaders, managers and front-line delivery teams will all certainly benefit from reading this thoughtfully crafted book."

–Josh Rab
Director of Product Management for TurboTax, Intuit

"Anyone can restate the obvious. Sean's approach makes you think, learn and grow. Don't forget to thank him later."

–Rick Gessner
Founder, Goju Labs

"Easy to Use 2.0 provides a detailed framework that captures a thoughtful and full-bodied approach to user experience considerations that must be addressed to ensure a proper research, design, testing, and delivery process. Beyond this guidance, the book also highlights and enforces the business justification behind investing in user experience by portraying the significant impact UX has on driving adoption, interaction, and ultimately revenue within any enterprise software business. This type of justification is imperative for any disruptor that's looking to effect change within a company."

–David Peck
Account Executive, Enterprise Corporate Sales, Salesforce.com

"In Easy to Use, Sean has defined a playbook and a robust framework for fitting design into the Agile Software Development process. The book is short, to the point and provides hands on, real-world examples to illustrate the success and common pitfalls of Agile UX. The hidden value of the book is that the techniques and information is just as valuable to Product Mangers, Project Managers, Developers, QA, and Business Analysts as it is to the UX professionals."

–Mukul Bisht,
Lead User Experience Designer, DocuSign

"Easy to Use 2.0 has been instrumental in helping to progress our teams' collaboration. The mantra of "a picture is worth a thousand words... and a prototype is worth a thousand meetings" has already saved us months' worth of time. Having a common language and understanding of the ramifications of Technical Debt and UX Debt have helped propel our team's communication to not only act fast but to also act strategically understanding the both near and long term objectives. I would highly recommend Easy to Use for anyone looking to take their User Experience to the next level!"

–Tom Wolfe
Cofounder of Thinking Engines

"You've heard that UX is good and needed at your company, but don't know where to start. Start here, where Sean Van Tyne breaks down the essentials — where UX came from, what it truly means, and provides a blue-print for applying its methods and tools."

–Phil Ohme
Design Strategist, Intuit

Easy to Use 2.0

ALSO BY SEAN VAN TYNE

The Customer Experience Revolution
(with Jeofrey Bean)

*The Guide to the Product Management
and Marketing Body of Knowledge*
(Contributor)

Human Centered Design
First International Conference, HCD 2009

EASY
TO USE
2.0

User Experience in Agile Development for
Enterprise Software

S e a n   V a n   T y n e

Crystal Pointe Media

Easy to Use 2.0:

User Experience in Agile Development for
Enterprise Software

Sean Van Tyne
Copyright 2017

ISBN-13: 978-1545283196

ISBN-10: 1545283192

Illustrations by Damon Mathews

Published by Crystal Pointe Media Inc.

San Diego, California

This book is dedicated to Laura and our girls
for which my life makes sense.

Contents

Foreword   XVII
Acknowledgements   XIX
Introduction   XXI

CHAPTER 1   1

What is User Experience?   1

Myth and Reality   1
   We Are in the Experience Economy   3
   What UX Is and Is Not   5
   In a Nutshell   7

CHAPTER 2   9

User Experience and Your Organization   9
   User Experience Maturity   10
   User Experience Strategy   15

UX Strategy Scorecard Workshops   17
   In a Nutshell   21

CHAPTER 3   23

User Experience Design and Agile Software
Development   23
   Agile Software Development   25
   User Experience in Agile Software Development 30
   Centralizing Design but Not Implementation   31

User Experience Design Process in Overall
Product Lifecycle   33
Agile UX   34
In a Nutshell   40

CHAPTER 4   41

UX Design Early in the Product Lifecycle   41
  Design Thinking, Minimal Viable Product and Minimal
  Desirable Product   44
  User Research   49
  Personas   55
  Scenarios, Activities and Tasks   57
  Iterative Design   61
  In a Nutshell   70

CHAPTER 5   71

Usability: Making Sure You Got It Right   71
  Usability Evaluations   72
  Accessibility   76
  Pre-Development Usability Evaluations   78
  Post Release Usability Evaluations   79
  In a Nutshell   83

CHAPTER 6   85

User Experience in Development   85

User Experience Collaboration with Development
89
UX Debt   91
In a Nutshell   96

CHAPTER 7   97

Building Your User Organization   97
In a Nutshell   107

Bibliography   108

About the Author   **111**

Foreword

Easy to Use is a book that every Agile product manager, designer and developer should have. The principals Sean shares in this book are sound, practical, and easy to use.

I have had the pleasure of working with Sean at multiple companies. I first met Sean when I was a product manager at Mitchell International. Sean was growing the User Experience team into a group that greatly helped us drive customer value into our product experiences. Sean developed partnerships across Product Management and Engineering to bridge the gap between product requirements and software specifications to deliver a solution to our customers that increased adoption, retention, advocacy and long-term sustainable revenue. Sean was one of the thought leaders to Mitchell's adoption of Agile and ensured UX was integrated properly from the beginning.

After I left Mitchell, I kept in touch with Sean as he continued to further refine his approach to integrating UX and Agile practices through his teaching and consulting work at other enterprise companies.

Later in my career I became the product management and UX design leader for a company that was investing heavily in our UX design team and practices. As we were dealing with challenges of scale and the melding of UX and Agile practices, I knew I needed to bring in someone who could help me set the team up for success, so I didn't hesitate to call Sean.

Sean was quickly able to assess the situation we were facing and started driving results immediately. His combination of UX, Agile and enterprise software knowledge, strategic leadership, and soft skills has empowered him to infuse measurable value into the teams that he works with. I have seen him effectively facilitate cross-departmental task forces to define and improve UX design in Agile operations. The teams he has worked with continue to leverage Sean on strategic initiatives and special projects.

Steve Mourton
Vice President, Product Management & UX Design
Sony Interactive Entertainment

Acknowledgements

Several good friends and colleagues help make this book possible. First and foremost, my best friend and partner for life, Laura, who puts up with me and keeps me honest, practical and, as best as she can, sane. Laura was also chief editor and provided endless hours of constructive feedback. It helps when your wife has a publishing company.

Jodi Tahsler was an outstanding editor. It is really the editor that shapes the book experience. This book is much better because of Jodi.

Armond Mehrarbian, a good friend, colleague and partner in many of these UX design and Agile development adventures, helped develop some of the examples from the first edition.

Steve Craig, fellow UX Boot Camp Leader, provided essential feedback. Damon Matthews, UX Boot Camp graduate, provide great feedback and did all the illustrations.

Alfonso de la Nuez, Co-Founder & CEO at UserZoom, helped with the descriptions of remote evaluations, moderated and unmoderated.

Rick Gessner, another great friend, colleague and all around amazing human being, helped with several of the ideas around MVP. I hope to write a book with Rick someday.

Introduction

As best as I can tell (and I have talked to most of the pioneers in our field about this), the term "User Experience" has been around since the 1980's. Some have credited its origins to Apple. Apple may have had the first User Experience team and Don Norman may have been the first User Experience Architect. Back then, User Experience was abbreviated "UE." I don't know exactly when it happened, but by the 1990's, it was more common to see the "UX" abbreviation we see today (Don has even given in and adopted the UX).

Regardless of its origins or abbreviation, User Experience – or UX – has grown from an obscure, nerdy concept for tech geeks to a mainstream practice that anyone designing anything for people pays attention to. Futurists in the 1990's predicted that our global economy would be based on experiences (Pine & Gilmore, 1999) and that Experience Makers would dominate the marketplaces (Bean & Van Tyne, 2012).

Well, they were right. We are living in the experience economy now, and I expect that it will be an experience economy for a while. Experience Makers like Apple have changed the way we think about computers, music, mobile communication and much more. Disney is an Experience Magician with armies of Imagineers designing our dream experiences. Even companies like Starbucks have changed the way that we think about an everyday, ordinary cup of coffee. Starbucks is our third dwelling place – home, work and Starbucks.

You see, experience design applied to everything from games, attractions, events, indoor and outdoor spaces, devices – and even software.

I was an artist and teacher in the 1980's and knew nothing of this UX thing. But in the 1990's I switched careers to technology – Information Technology (IT), database architecture, network architecture…and then this internet thing started to capture my interest. A perfect marriage between my love for art, education and technology, web development and design was immediate. You didn't have to wait for any program to compile or run. A blend of visual design, interaction design and the need to make something easy to understand…easy to interact…easy to use.

Along my UX journey, I have a learned a few things. This book covers the things I have learned around user experience, agile development and enterprise software. Come along with me, and I will share ideas and concepts that you can apply today to your UX journey.

Sean Van Tyne
www.SeanVanTyne.com

CHAPTER 1

What is User Experience?
Myth and Reality

"User Experience encompasses all aspects of the end-user's interaction with the company, its services, and its products."

– The Nielsen Norman Group

Don Norman is most often credited for coining the term User Experience while at Apple in the 1980's – having started what is believed to be the first User Experience group. Don also wrote *The Design of Everyday Things* (Norman, 2002), that provides us with the Principles of User-Centered Design (or Human-Centered Design) that we follow today.

The Nielsen Norman Group – with Principals Jakob Nielsen, Don Norman and Bruce Tognazzini – defines *User Experience* as "encompass[ing] all aspects of the end-user's interaction with the company, its services, and its products." (Nielsen Norman) You could say that User Experience is a natural evolution from Human-Computer Interaction from Human-Machine Interaction from Human Factors. Essentially, it has been around forever but no one ever gave it a name. The focus, as defined by Neilson Normal Group, is on "the **end-user's** interaction with the company, its services, and its products."

This is a broad definition of user experience. Many Experience Design-leading organizations have a leader for experience like a Chief Design Officer, Senior Vice President of UX, or similar title that oversees their customers' experience across their brand, products and services. But most software companies are not that sophisticated, and user experience is thought of as more of a process associated with developing the software. According to Apple Development the user experience for *applications* "encompasses the visual appearance, interactive behavior, and assistive capabilities of software..." (Apple). This is a focus on the visual design, interaction design, usability and accessibility of the software.
The overall goal of designing experiences for

enterprise software is to take the inherent complexity and make it simple for the end-users. The one overarching principle is to make it easy and obvious to do the right thing and hard or impossible to do the wrong thing. That may sound easy, but it is not. There are many things to consider when designing experiences for enterprise software. Enterprise software, by its definition, is large, complex and serves many different types of people (end-users). It is hard to be easy.

We Are in the Experience Economy

Joseph Pine II and James H. Gilmore published *Welcome to the Experience Economy* for the *Harvard Business Review* (Pine & Gilmore, 1998) followed by the book, *The Experience Economy: Work Is Theater & Every Business a Stage* (Pine & Gilmore, 1998). Pine and Gilmore provide us with the first description of the new economy that we are in today, the Experience Economy, as the natural evolution to follow the agrarian economy, the industrial economy, and the recent service economy.

Pine and Gilmore outline how leading organizations orchestrate memorable events for their customers, and theorize that the memory itself becomes the product – the "experience." More advanced experience organizations, Experience Makers, charge for the value of the "transformation" that an experience offers.

The best Experience Makers know that great experiences can change people's lives and revolutionize marketplaces. At the highest level, transformations make a permanent beneficial change to a person. While experiences are memorable and are sustained for a time, *transformations* are inspirational and are sustained through time.

Think of coffee, for example. You can buy and trade coffee as a commodity and make a decent margin if all is going well. You could also take those coffee beans and bag them up as a product and sell them for a better margin. You can brew that coffee and serve it in a diner or restaurant and – combined with the service – make even more margin. Or you could build an experience around the coffee: make the place that you purchase and drink the coffee a destination – an experience – and you can now charge a premium price for that coffee. That is exactly what Starbucks did.
Companies that do this are Experience Makers and they dominate their marketplace by

elevating a transaction to an experience. Think of what Disney did to amusement parks; Apple did to the phone; Amazon did to internet shopping and Netflix did to renting movies. Look at what is happening with mobile, cloud subscription-based economy from travel to finance. The winners in these new marketplaces with be the ones that deliver the best experience. And that is just as true with enterprise software.

What UX Is and Is Not

There are many misconceptions about what UX is that we want to clear up. User Experience is not just User Interface. User Interface – or UI – refers to human interaction with a computer or other software devices. User experience is much broader than just the human-computer or human-machine interaction. There are parts of the user experience that take place before, after and around the UI that must be consider when looking at the experience your software delivers.

UX is not just usability. Usability refers to the ease of use and learnability of a human-made object such as a tool or device. Usability is about how effective, efficient, and satisfactory an experience is. This is an important aspect of UX but is not all that UX is. Your software may be easy to use but not aesthetically pleasing. Or it may fulfill its function but not make the user feel they can't live without it. There is an emotional component to how we use and experience things.

UX is not just design. Design is a process. Design is usually focused on aesthetics and function. It, too, is an important part of UX but is not UX. You could develop a beautiful screen that is not easy to understand or in the wrong context of the overall experience.

UX encompasses user interface, usability, design and more. Messaging, for example, is a part of the user experience. Training and billing are a part of the user experience. Even troubleshooting is part of UX. Every interaction with an organization, its brand, its message, its services, and its products – everything that a user can experience is the user experience.

In a Nutshell

✓ User Experience encompasses all aspects of the end-user's interaction with the company, its services, and its products.

✓ We are living in the Experience Economy, and Experience Makers change people's lives and revolutionize marketplaces. The winners in these new marketplaces will be the ones that deliver the best experience. And that is just as true with enterprise software.

✓ The user experience for *applications* encompasses the visual appearance, interactive behavior, usability and assistive capabilities of software.

✓ The overall goal of designing experiences for enterprise software is to take the inherent complexity and make it simple for the end-users. The one overarching principle is to make it easy and obvious to do the right thing and hard or impossible to do the wrong thing.

CHAPTER 2

User Experience and Your Organization

"Your customers are having an experience with your brand, product and services regardless if you are consciously managing it."

– Sean Van Tyne

A good user experience delights your customers – increasing adoption, retention, loyalty and, ultimately, revenue. A poor user experience detracts your customers, drives them to your competition and, eventually, your products and services are no longer a viable source of revenue. As organizations become more aware of their user experience, they develop processes to architect, manage and measure it – and reap the benefits.

User Experience Maturity

User experience management varies from organizations that are just becoming aware of the concepts of user experience to organizations where user experience is one of, if not the, core distinction. A UX maturity model is a framework that describes an organization's maturity along a continuum. It provides a clear path to reach the next level and a benchmark for relative comparison of organizations.

As mentioned above, organizations' products and services have a "user experience" regardless if they are aware of it. Organizations that manage and measure their user experience process gain the revenue benefits. The User Experience Maturity Model (Figure 2-1) helps organizations understand where they are along the continuum and what they need to do to advance to the next level of maturity.

There are five levels defined along the continuum of user experience maturity. Organizations progress through a sequence of stages as their user experience management processes evolve and mature.

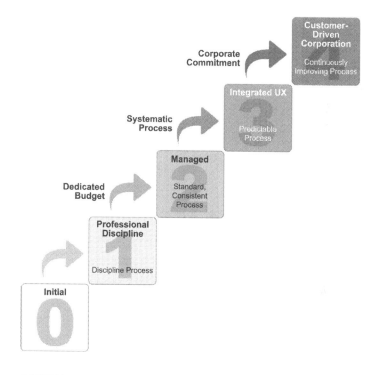

FIGURE 2-1: The User Experience Maturity Model

Level 0: Initial Stage

We don't know what we don't know. An organization may not be aware of the concept of user experience or understands its benefits. In this initial stage, someone shares this knowledge and a grass root effort begins. This could be a simple heuristic review to determine areas for improvement and executing to capture "low hanging fruit" - investments that yield immediate benefits – or bringing in an expert to suggest simple changes to a process or design that can yield big returns in increased efficiency, effectiveness or satisfaction.

At this stage, it is typically undocumented and driven in a reactive manner by users' dissatisfaction. Not all the stakeholders or participants may know that the effort is even taking place. The effort is likely to depend heavily on the knowledge and efforts of relatively few people or small groups.

If successful, this effort may capture that low-hanging fruit and show benefits which will lead to bringing in a professional in a UX discipline.

Level 1: Professional Discipline

Once user experience is adopted as a professional discipline, then some user experience processes are repeatable with consistent results. The organization may adopt wireframes as a part of their discovery or definition process and find that it reduces cycle time in requirement analysis with development. Maybe they find that conducting a usability evaluation identified easy changes that increased end-user effectiveness, efficiency and satisfaction, which increased adoption and retention (and revenue).

The user experience activities newly introduced to the processes may not repeat for all the projects in the organization at this stage, but advocates may use some basic activities to track cost and benefits to start capturing return on investment (ROI).

At this stage, the minimum user experience process discipline is in place to repeat earlier successes on projects with similar applications and scope. Project status may now include user experience deliverables to management like completion of major user experience tasks and activities at major milestones.

Consistent positive results from integrated user experience activities may promote a dedicated budget and the formation of a user experience group that develops consistent processes that lead to the next level.

Level 2: Managed Process
When the user experience is managed, there are documented standards and process oversight. They establish consistent performance across projects. Projects apply standards, tailored, if necessary, within similarly guidelines. Upper management may establish and mandate these user experience standards for the organization's

set of standard processes.

The user experience roles, activities and artifacts may be integrated into some of the organization's processes. User experience resources and tasks may be added to template project plans.

Measured results and ROI may capture the attention of executive management. The organization may decide that user experience must now be considered in their overall corporate strategy.

Level 3: Integrated User Experience

When an organization integrates user experience into their corporate strategy then, using metrics, they can effectively control their customers' user experience with their products and services. In level three, the organization identifies ways to adjust and adapt the process to a project and tailors it to fit the needs of the target market, segmentation and customer type.

Quantitative quality user experience goals become part of the overall corporate balanced scorecard. The organization's financial perspective to increase revenue, increasing customer satisfaction in the customer perspective by measuring the product's usability score in the process perspective, becomes a part of the User Experience Scorecard.

If a focus on user experience becomes a core distinction for an organization, then they may enter the highest level of corporate user experience maturity.

Level 4: Customer-Driven Corporation

If one of the primary focuses of the organization is on continually improving the user experience process, then the organization has become customer-driven in a controlled and measured way. The user experience objectives become core to the organization and are annually reviewed and revised to reflect changing market and business objectives. This may include having user experience professionals involved in corporate strategies such as participating in discovering and defining new market segments or participating in third-party vendor selection in terms of the overall corporate user experience integration.

User Experience Strategy

There are entire books dedicated to the topic of user experience strategy. In context of user experience in agile development for enterprise applications, there are a few basics that we need to cover.

A user experience strategy is a plan of action to achieve your brand, product or service experience objectives. Your user experience strategy is built around how it contributes to your overall organization's business objectives. This may be measured against customer adoption, retention, loyalty or advocacy or increasing your customers' efficiency or reducing training or support calls. How does your user experience help increase revenue or reduce cost? Whatever is important to your organization's strategy, your user experience strategy must be aligned.

Your user experience strategy usually boils down to what is perceived as user-friendly, intuitive or easy to use by your customers. There may be many perspectives in your organization on what makes your brand, products or services delightful to your customers. Do not get caught in the trap of thinking "I know what our customers want." There is a simple process to determine for certain what your customers consider easy to use. Let data drive your decisions. Use quantitative and qualitative findings inform your strategy. Surveys, interviews, observations, support call logs, web analytics and more can inform your decision-making process.

The other part of a good user experience strategy is presenting it to your target audience in a way that makes sense to them. Know what is important to the strategic decision makers in your organization and present your strategy in terms that are important to them. If your leaders are interested in increasing revenue, then show how your user experience strategy is going to increase revenue – maybe by increasing customer adoption or retention or loyalty or advocacy. If your organization is focused on reducing cost, then show how your user experience strategy will reduce discovery for development, testing and training or how it will reduce support calls or training. Whatever your organization's strategy, align your user experience strategy for acceptance, adoption and further investment.

UX Strategy Scorecard Workshops

One of the things that I like to do to help companies understand their UX maturity and develop their UX strategic objectives and Key

Performance Indicators (KPI) is to conduct a workshop. The workshop can be a few hours to a few days depending on the size and maturity of the organization.

If it is a large organization, I will do a 360 review for the organization or department that we are developing the scorecard for. I will interview key contributors within the department and key stakeholders that work with the department. From the interviews, we can gain perspective into how the department perceives its strengths and weaknesses compared to their outside stakeholders' perceptions. We can also look at this by product line, service group, value stream or whatever grouping perspective has the most value to help determine our objectives and KPIs.

If is a small organization, then we can get everyone involved to sit around the table and work this out in real-time.

The goal is to put your experience design solutions into the context of the market problems they solve, the business objectives they support, and the customer and user needs they meet. Using a scorecard helps organizations balance and achieve their strategic objectives across financial, customer, process and resource perspectives.

For example, if a financial objective is to increase revenue, the related customer objective may be to increase adoption and/or loyalty and/or advocacy. The related process objective for UX may be to conduct more iterative design reviews with customers to ensure that they are delighted to adopt and be a loyal advocate. From a resource perspective, you may need to hire more people to make prototypes and run reviews.

In a session, we will review strengths and opportunities and derive objectives that address these. We group the objectives by the four perspectives in a scorecard. We then determine how we want to measure each objective, the metrics that we are going to use and the initiatives that will achieve it.

For example, with a financial objective like increase revenue, you may measure net profit with a target of 5% annual growth with an action plan initiative. You may measure customer satisfaction with a survey and target a specific rating. A common UX measure is usability test results with a 70% pass rate.

At the end of the session, we will have alignment with the User Experience strategy and KPI with the overall company strategy and business measures. This clarity helps an organization to manage growth and helps employees to understand how their everyday work contributes to the organization's overall goals.

In a Nutshell

✓ Your customers are having an experience with your brand, product and services regardless if you are consciously managing it.

✓ A good user experience delights your customers – increasing adoption, retention, loyalty and, ultimately, revenue, and a poor user experience detracts your customers, drives them to your competition and, eventually, your products and services are no longer a viable source of revenue.

✓ Organizations that manage and measure their user experience process gain the revenue benefits.

✓ A UX maturity model is a framework that describes an organization's maturity along a continuum and provides a clear path to reach the next level and a benchmark for relative comparison of organizations.

✓ A user experience strategy is a plan of action to achieve your brand, product and service experience objectives and contributes to your overall organization's business objectives

CHAPTER 3

User Experience Design and Agile Software Development

"In preparing for battle I have always found that plans are useless, but planning is indispensable."

– Dwight D. Eisenhower

Enterprise software is only easy to use if your customers and users think it is easy to use. To determine "ease of use" you must understand your customer and user needs. For enterprise solutions, the customer is usually someone in management interested in finding the best way to bring efficiency to their operation, whereas the user is typically an employee more interested in completing their daily assignments as easily and effectively as possible. The customer is looking at the overall workflow of their organization and how specific solutions might improve it, whereas the user tends to emphasize the solution's ease of use.

For a consumer experience, the customer is the buyer that is making the purchasing decision while the recipient of the purchase – product and/or service – is the user. For example, if I was purchasing flowers online for my wife, I would be the buyer making the purchase decisions. There is a series of decisions that I would make along my journey – where I want to make my purchase, what products and services I want, payment, delivery, etc. My wife is the user. She would experience the delivery and out-of-box experience, (hopefully) enjoy the product itself, etc.

Determining, developing and deploying enterprise software is a collaborative, multi-discipline, cross-functional endeavor. User experience professionals conduct research, work with internal subject matter experts and evaluate designs with clients to understand the market, customer and users' needs to design solutions that are easy to use.

Agile Software Development

The agile methodology is based on iterative and incremental development cycles where requirements and solutions evolve through collaboration between self-organizing, cross-functional teams. According to the Agile Manifesto, agile software development values:

- Individuals and Interactions Over Processes and Tools
- Working Software Over Comprehensive Documentation
- Customer Collaboration Over Contract Negotiation
- Responding to Change Over Following a Plan

Individuals and Interactions Over Processes and Tools

This does not mean that agile software development does not value process and tools but it realizes that individuals and interactions are more important to develop software successfully. You may have the best processes and tools in the world, but it is the individuals and their interaction that make it successful.

Having an effective, efficient process that is clearly understood and the right tools to do your job is still necessary but means nothing without effective individual interactions.

In enterprise software solutions, user experience is a part of the collaborative, multi-disciplined, cross-functional team interactions. UX professionals participate in the product lifecycle process. UX brings their best practice process and tools to enhance the overall lifecycle.

In his book, *What the CEO Wants You to Know* (Charan, 2001), Ram Charan explains that "A leader of the business knows what to do. A leader of the people knows how to get it done." Business acumen provides the roadmap and clarity, but the ability to link people's actions and decisions to the right priorities is what make successful organizations.

Working Software Over Comprehensive Documentation

This does not mean that agile software development does not value documentation but it realizes that working software is the goal. Documentation can be reduced with more individual interactions. As teams interact less or there is higher turnover in team members then more documentation is needed to communicate the solution's requirements.

The same is true of UX collaboration. With multi-disciplined UX resources integrated into product teams, the right balance of UX documentation must be applied for each product release team's needs.

If your team is small enough to sit in the same room and look each other in the face every day, then you probably can get away with little or no documentation. But as your team grows and daily face-to-face interaction becomes more challenging, then you need documentation to cover the communication gap.

To keep everyone on the same page, there needs to be a page to be on. As a UX designer, I think about what is the quickest and most concise way to communicate the design to my target audience. Is it wireframes, PowerPoint or sitting in a room with a whiteboard and taking a picture of that? A picture is worth a thousand words…and a prototype is worth a thousand meetings.

For Agile documentation, we need documentation to be lean, meaningful, crisp and to the point.

Customer Collaboration Over Contract Negotiation

From a software development perspective, it is more important to understand the customer's needs than what was negotiated in the contract. To develop software that meets customer needs requires regular communication with the customer all along the development process (and prior to the development process and after development).

If you are a small software company or you are working in a design partnership with your customers, then customer collaboration is the actual customer who is purchasing your solution.

If you are a large organization, the customer may be your internal customer representative – for example, product management. In a daily stand-up, the Product Owner represents your customer.

When it comes to today's marketplace, it is more important than ever to understand the customer's needs. Customer collaboration is especially key to determining, developing and deploying a successful experience design for your customers and end-users. UX professionals collaborate with customers and customer representatives early and often throughout the lifecycle of a product. Ensure that your UX professionals – either internal or external resources – are involved early and often in defining and designing your solution.

Responding to Change Over Following a Plan

Benjamin Franklin said, "If you fail to plan, you plan to fail." In today's quickly changing markets, successful organizations need to adapt at a more rapid pace. You must have a plan to succeed but in today's modern software marketplace, you must have plans that are flexible enough to support last-minute changes.

Flexible plans, iterative development and collaboration are the cornerstone of the user experience design process, too. To determine that the experience meets the organization's business needs and delight the customer, UX continuously reviews concepts, designs and user interactions with key customers and stakeholders throughout the solution's lifecycle. Research insights inform the iterative design process and usability evaluation cycle. Just-in-time design requirements provide direction to the Agile development iterations.

Another way to think about this is: plans don't fail; people fail to plan. Having no plan is worse than having a bad plan. At least with a bad plan you have something to improve. In the rapidly changing world that we live in today, we need to plan and our plans need to be agile.

User Experience in Agile Software Development

A common challenge in Agile Software Development is how to incorporate user experience best practices into a rapid iterative and incremental development process. Attempting to resolve complex user interactions while trying to code and test incremental deliverables at the same time does not work. And running usability tests cannot occur for the iteration that is also attempting to complete the same functionality that needs to be tested. Interaction design and usability testing must be planned in advanced of the iteration for that functionality.

Having the user experience tasks track ahead of development allows the time needed to validate the customer and end-users' needs are met. It does not add time to the schedule because these tasks happen parallel to other project tasks. The key is ensuring that the experience designs are effective, efficient and delightful to your customers and end-users just-in-time for the development iteration that will be implementing it.

Centralizing Design but Not Implementation

Designing a system's experience is a holistic endeavor akin to architecture. You must consider the total experience in context of the end-to-end interactions of the system. The broader strokes must be planned and understood early in the product lifecycle while the details of the design may be determined, developed and deployed in an iterative fashion. Especially for large-scale, enterprise solutions, a centralized design team ensures that style guides, interaction guidelines and a standard user interface component library is adhered to for a consistent, effective and efficient experience. The larger the effort and more complex the solution, the greater the need for a centralized design team. Not having a centralized UX team puts consistency, the clients' satisfaction and the related costs and revenue at risk.

Though the team is centralized to maintain consistency across the product portfolio, UX resources must be integrated into the product teams to best meet the individual product's specific market, customer and end-user needs. Each product and service has unique needs that a dedicated UX resource must have a deep understanding of to design the experience in context of these target customers and end-users while being mindful of the general UX standard guidelines across the portfolio.

Conduct Iterative Reviews Early and Often

Conduct iterative reviews with your customers early and often to reduce uncertainty and risk. The agile methodology values customer collaboration and is key to user experience best practices. Conduct reviews as early and as often as possible in the product lifecycle to vet assumptions and validate design direction. It is fast and cheap to validate early concepts and initial designs. The earlier you can validate the design, the greater the return on investment in cost saving for development and satisfaction, adoption and retention with customers and increased revenue.

User Experience Design Process in Overall Product Lifecycle

User experience activities take place early in the overall product lifecycle. The user experience design is determined along with the vision, architecture and feature set; developed along with the release planning and features; and delivered in the developed, tested and released version of the software. There are three major activities of user experience:

User Research – Analysis of current solutions and competition to understand users' behavior, needs and motivations

Iterative Design – Reviews with internal subject matter experts and clients to validate design solutions delights the customer

Usability Evaluation – Evaluations with end-users to ensure that the interaction is effective, efficient and delightful

Research and some high-level design are done as early as possible in the product lifecycle. More detailed designs and evaluations iterate ahead of development. It is important that all the major UX design activities are completed before the development iterations begin so that there are no questions about the experience design and the focus is on developing working software.

Agile UX

Agile UX focuses on the experience being designed using rapid techniques. This method shows that collaborating closely with other members of the product team and gathering feedback early and often produces positive results in a timely manner. Driving the design in short, iterative cycles to assess what works best for the business and the user, Agile UX shows us how to make these changes for faster, better outcomes. Tenets of Agile UX include:

- Frame a vision of the problem you're solving and focus your team on the right outcomes.
- Share your insights with your team much earlier in the process.
- Create minimal viable and desirable products to determine which ideas are valid.
- Incorporate the voice of the customer throughout the process.
- Integrate UX with Agile development frameworks.

By providing insight into the design work to your teammates sooner rather than further down the design road, you accomplish the following:

1. Ensure that you're aligned with the broader team and the business vision.
2. Give developers a sneak peek at the direction of the application (speeding up development and surfacing challenges earlier).
3. Further flesh out your thinking, since verbalizing your concepts to others forces you to focus on areas that you didn't think of when you were pushing the pixels.

The trick is to stay agile: keep the deliverables light and editable. Eliminate waste by not spending hours getting the pixels exactly right and the annotations perfect. Got an idea for a flow? Throw it up on the whiteboard, and grab the product owner or project leader to tell them about it. Ready to design? Rough out the first page of the flow in your sketchpad. How does it feel? Is the flow already evident? Post it in a visible place at the office and invite passers-by to comment on it. Grab people from the hallway and get their feedback.

Integrating UX into Agile Development

Over the years, I have helped many enterprise software organizations better integrate user experience design into their agile development process. There are two fundamental concepts that must be understood: Agile iterations are focused on developing and testing the software, and user experience design is a holistic approach to defining the software experience.

The first thing to recognize is that Agile is a development process, and user experience, in terms of software development, is focused on the visual and interaction design and usability and accessibility of the software. In the Agile development iteration, we are focused on the development and testing of the software in that iteration, which means that everything a software developer and tester needs to do their job for their iteration must be provided before they begin their iteration. There are some things that we will not know until we start development but, for the most part, the software requirements for each iteration must be well thought out in context of the overall final software product and business objectives. The same is true for the experience design.

The experience design must consider the overall holistic experience – end-to-end. The end-users will interact to provide proper instruction for each development iteration. There may be some discovery in the development iteration about implementing the experience design – challenges that were not anticipated or better ways of displaying the content. This is all expected in the agile process. In fact, this is part of the power of agile – to fail fast, learn fast, and quickly adapt.

Once an organization understands that agile development is an iterative process for developing and testing the software and that experience design is a holistic process that provides design requirements for each iteration, then we can begin on the right path.

The second thing is to plan your experience design as part of your software requirements. Experience designing doesn't happen in an iteration. It must be well thought out in advance. Just like we test our software code, we test our user experience designs. The design must be tested (to some degree) prior to each development iteration. Before it can be tested, the design must be developed – just like the code. Before it can be developed, it must be defined – just like the code. The defining, development and testing of the design must iterate ahead of the development iteration just like the other software requirements.

How an organization plans their experience design is up to them. There are many factors to consider – time to market, technological capabilities, budget, business goals and more. Understanding the need to plan and iterate ahead of development is the key to successfully integrate user experience in agile development.

In a Nutshell

✓ Enterprise software is only easy to use if your customers and users think it is easy to use.

✓ User experience professionals conduct research, work with internal subject matter experts and evaluate designs with clients to understand the market, customer and users' needs to design solutions that are easy to use.

✓ The Agile methodology is based on iterative and incremental development cycles where requirements and solutions evolve through collaboration between self-organizing, cross-functional teams.

✓ The Agile method values: Individuals and Interactions Over Processes and Tools; Working Software Over Comprehensive Documentation; Customer Collaboration Over Contract Negotiation; and Responding to Change Over Following a Plan.

✓ Agile UX focuses on the experience being designed using rapid techniques and lightweight deliverables.

CHAPTER 4

UX Design Early in the Product Lifecycle

*"You can use an eraser on the
drawing table or a sledge hammer
on the construction site."*

— *Frank Lloyd Wright*

In large-scale agile development, the vision is defined along with the architecture and feature sets for the software over multiple releases. The vision, architecture and feature sets inform the UX design direction. UX Research and some high-level design are done at this time to determine the overall UX design direction of the software.

This is a collaborative effort across multi-disciplined, cross-functional teams. Product Marketing and Management work with Sales,

Marketing and other stakeholders to help determine the business opportunities. Engineering and related disciplines are responsible for the delivery of the solutions while user experience is an important part of the team that defines the customers' interaction. In some organizations, the Chief Experience Officer is a part of the executive team that leads this. In other organizations, a senior level Experience Manager is a part of the Portfolio Management team, while other organizations may have an upper management UX leader as part of the Architecture team to help define the solution's experience in context of the business opportunities.

At this point in the process, the focus is to align the vision, architecture and high-level features with the investment themes. The UX research and high-level design help determine the investment themes, vision, architecture and feature set through research and high-level design activities. At the beginning of this phase, the participants (UX, Arch, PM, etc.) present a unified vision of what the teams need to build for the next incremental release. UX designs are a visual elaboration of the written business requirements.

In agile development, we create user stories to

communicate the software requirements. A user story is a sentence in the language of the end-user that captures what they want to do to accomplish their goal. It captures the *who*, *what* and *why* of a requirement.

For example:

As a <who>, **I want** <what> **so that** <why>
As a <role>, **I want** <goal> **so that** <benefit>
As an <actor> **I want** <action> **so that** <achievement>

Epic stories are large user stories that communicate a bigger vision. Epic stories are too big to implement in a single iteration and are broken down into smaller user stories for development.

For example, let's say we are designing an enterprise solution where one of the requirements is to allow the client to add and maintain their users independent of their IT department. The task must be easy enough for a business user to add, delete and edit users without IT assistance.

The vision for this may be "We need to give business managers the ability to add new users to the enterprise application so that they can be maintained and configured without assistance from the IT staff. This will allow IT budgets to be slashed by 20%."

And the epic story for this may be "As a supervisor, I want the ability to add new users to the system so that I can more easily and quickly grant access to my team members and make them productive."

Design Thinking, Minimal Viable Product and Minimal Desirable Product

Tim Brown and IDEO have been leading the charge on an innovation model built around Design Thinking (Brown, 2009). In this model, there are three key perspectives:

Viability. Is it viable? Is it capable of producing a profit or achieving your goal? Does it have a reasonable chance of succeeding?

Feasibility. Is it feasible? What is functionally possible in the foreseeable future? Does the technology exist or can it be created so that it can accomplish this at a reasonable cost or in an acceptable amount of time?

Desirability. Is it desired? Is there a market for it? Does anyone want this or need this? What makes sense to people and for people?

Viability is a business-focused discussion around marketing and finance. This requires an analytical discussion around the business, rather than the core user experience itself. Financial metrics and market sizes become the dominating point of discussion. It predicts what is likely to be possible in a sustainable business model.

Feasibility is an engineering-focused discussion around platforms, architecture, process, skills and tools. Does the technology exist today to accomplish what you need or can you develop the technology you need with reasonable cost and time? Desirability is a design-focused discussion around customers, aesthetics, function and form. For design-focused products, the focus might be on:

- context, culture, and goals
- customer goals and product experience
- design aesthetics and interactions

Here is where we ask the question: "How do we improve the current experience, or do we create a whole new experience?" The tools employed at this initial stage might include user research, development of personas and user goals, journey maps and rapid prototyping to explore concepts.

A Minimal Viable Product (MVP) is a product with just enough features to gather validated learning about the product and its continued development. Gathering insights from an MVP is often less expensive than developing a product with more features, which increase costs and risk if the product fails, for example, due to incorrect assumptions.

The point of the MVP is to get a read on viability as early as possible, maybe before you build anything.

Minimum – smallest possible thing
Viable – provable by a set of legit customers

that match your personas
Product – a promised solution that "does a job" for a paying customer

The most-MVP thing possible then, is just an idea. If you can get strangers to give you a check today so you can start building a product that solves their "job to be done," you've won the MVP challenge.

A Minimum Desirable Product (MDP) approach focuses primarily on whether you are providing a great product experience that creates value for your customers.

Business-driven organizations may assess viability up front, thinking about metrics and revenue and market sizes. A feasibility (engineering) oriented organization may start with technology first, then build a business around it. And a desirability-focused organization may focus on the target customer, their context and behavior, and build a product experience around that.

Where MVP is the version of a new product that brings back the maximum amount of validated learning about your customers with the least effort, MDP is the version of a product that qualifies the interest in it and the need for its existence. The risk with MVP is that it kick starts customer development before you even have customers. A Desirability-First strategy includes:

- Understanding user goals
- Creating a Minimum Desirable Product
- Listening to users and maximizing love
- Iterating to a great product experience

All three perspectives are important – Viability, Feasibility and Desirability. If it is not capable of producing a profit or achieving your goal, then it is not viable. If the technology does not exist or it cannot be created at a reasonable cost or in an acceptable amount of time, then it is not feasible. But if no one wants or needs it, then why bother?

User experience is all about what is desirable, ensuring that your software solution is desirable in the context of viability and feasibility. Early user research is done in a rapid way to vet these issues early in the process so time and resources are not wasted.

User Research

Henry Ford once said, "If I had asked people what they wanted, they would have said faster horses." The same is true for developing enterprise solutions. When designing your user experience, it is important to note that, in most cases, your customers and users don't know what they want...specifically. They know that they want efficient, effective solutions and have some ideas about how to improve the workflow, but it is up to the software solution provider to be able to bridge the gap between the customer and user needs and the technology solution that meets that need.

For example, some customers may already have an existing directory service that provides their Lightweight Directory Access Protocol (LDAP) that your solution must integrate with to add their users. Other clients may have no LDAP solution, so you will need to provide them with one. Your product's user management solution will need to support various LDAP scenarios across your market.

The best solutions are usually something that customers and the users have never thought of. The real value that the software solution provider brings is the ability to interpret their market, customer and user needs and deliver a solution that is better than they could imagine because of the expertise that they bring in understanding their needs and the solutions that enterprise software can provide. Looking at previous solutions or workflows that satisfied the market may no longer apply. In many cases with innovation, you may find a solution in another market that you adapt to your solution – like Apple adding touchscreen technology to smartphones. Your research may include investigating the market, competition, customers and users of the market that the solution comes from and extrapolating from there.

For example, for your user management system, you may have a list of features like:

- View users
- Add users to the system
- Assign roles to users
- Delete users

- Edit users

As you review your current customers' solutions and other solutions in the market, you may add other features like:

- Adding role-based permissions
- Creating a system to notify users once their account is created
- Granting user access to update their profile
- Adding/deleting users within the appropriate hierarchy in the organizational structure so they can approve/disapprove purchases

As we progress from discovery to inception and elaboration of the requirements, user experience researchers vet assumptions by analyzing the market, competition and current release of your software. To design user experiences that are easy to use for your customers and users, you must become familiar with the customers' workflows and the users' tasks. When conducting your research, you must establish a list of users by companies, departments and roles. The company contact is usually the "customer" and the department contact is usually a manager. In enterprise software, there are customers that purchase the solution, users who use the system and managers who work for the customer and manage the users.

Include the managers in your research. Often the managers are also users – usually using the application for operational reports. The managers have insight into their employees' tasks, such as what positions are changing roles and tasks or being eliminated. Your solution is most likely going to change or eliminate their roles – this is not something you want to discuss with the user but should discuss with the managers. Sometimes it is the manager's role that is changing. In this case, you need to work with the right level of the customers' company to ensure this understanding.

For example, in the case of the user management solution, it will eliminate the business users' reliance on their IT department. This is good for the business in general, but the IT department may not be happy with giving up this control.

Survey, interview and observe the customers and users using their current solution. Develop diagrams of the various customers' workflows and note where they are similar and different. Group your customer and user types by similar roles and create personas – archetypes that synthesize their skills, patterns and goals to better understand their needs.

User Experience Researchers may review the current solutions that customers are using and the competition. This analysis helps vet assumptions about current solutions in the marketplace. User experience research analysis helps product teams form a clear vision for the product by defining the customers' and users' activities in context of the market problem the solution is solving. Markets are "made up" of segments. UX helps to define the market segmentations in terms of their needs in context of the problems that are being solved for them. UX research defines the strengths and weaknesses of the competition's solution compared to your solution along with how the various customers' goals, process workflows, activities and tasks are similar and different. Remember that innovation sometimes means looking at a solution in other markets and adapting it to another. The solution's vision provides the direction for the product's design.

The product team must follow the vision and not be afraid to ignore findings. Yes, listen to customers, but know when the findings support the vision. UX vet assumptions, validates design concepts with customers, and evaluates the solution with customers' end-users. Review market segmentation demographic data and interview stakeholders, customers and users to gain insight into their goals. A goal is a result one is attempting to achieve. UX observes the customers and users using the solution in their environment and develops diagrams of the various customers' workflows, noting where the goals and underlining activities are similar and different.

Quantitative and Qualitative Research

Qualitative research is used to gain understanding of underlying reasons, opinions and motivations. It provides insights into the problem and/or helps to develop ideas or hypotheses while quantitative research uses measurable data to formulate facts and uncover patterns. In the case of user experience research, we are interested in the end-users' reasoning and motivation – their mental model.

Qualitative data collection methods vary using unstructured or semi-structured techniques. Some common methods for qualitative research include focus groups (group discussions), individual interviews, and participation and observations. The sample size for qualitative research is typically small, which is great for quick studies in an agile process. Quantitative data collection methods tend to be more structured than qualitative data collection methods and require larger sample sizes but can be done quickly with automation.

In some cases, you may start with a quantitative method like a survey then follow up with a qualitative method like interviewing to get more insight. But it is more common to start with qualitative research to form a hypothesis then test the hypothesis with quantitative research to validate or invalidate the hypothesis and move on – fail fast – learn fast – and quickly adapt.

Personas

To develop a better understanding of the market, customers and end-users, UX Designers create buyer and user personas (Figure 4-1). Personas are a stand-in for a group of people who share common goals. They are fictional representatives—archetypes based on behaviors and attitudes. Buyer personas focus on the goals of the people who make the purchase decision for the software while user personas focus on the goals of the people who use the software.

Personas are usually developed from data collected from interviews with users, analytics gathered from system interaction and/or third-party research. They include descriptions of behaviors, goals, skills, attitudes and the working environment, with a few fictional personal details to make the persona a realistic character. For each product, more than one persona is usually created, but one persona should always be the primary focus for the design.

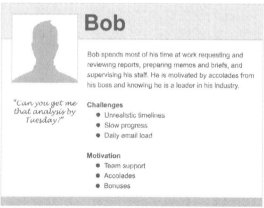

FIGURE 4-1: Persona example

The personas typically have names like "Bob" or "Sandy." Everyone involved in determining, developing and deploying the solution should have an intimate understanding of the personas. They typically have conversations like "Bob would never do that" or "Sandy would do this first then that." Personas are a great tool to connect the people who are designing and developing the solution with the people that are buying and using it.

For example, for your user management system, you may have a persona for Bob, a Senior Manager, who is interesting in viewing the users within the appropriate hierarchy in the organizational structure that can approve/disapprove purchases. Or Sandy, the Business Analyst, who will be updating the users in the system as they change departments or leave the company.

Scenarios, Activities and Tasks

Once the various roles and goals are understood (defined?) through the personas, UX works with product teams to think through the scenarios needed to realize the goals.

Scenarios describe a user's interaction with the solution. Scenarios are useful to define business cases and inform the user interaction design.

UX then determines what activities are needed to complete the goals by roles. An activity is a specific behavior or grouping of tasks. UX develops diagrams that illustrate the activities. An activity diagram shows activities and actions to describe workflows.

Activity diagrams divide the activities into tasks needed to complete the user's objective. A task is a unit of work. The task itself may be a single step in the process or multiple steps or sub-tasks that make up the task. Activity diagrams, sometimes called process flow diagrams (Figure 4-2), divide the scenario tasks as needed to convey what the user needs to do to complete their goal.

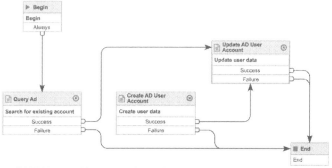

FIGURE 4-2: Process flow diagram example

For example, for our user management solution, we will need to understand the workflow of adding a user. This diagram can be as simple or as complex as needed to support the design needs.

Tasks analysis looks at tasks as outcomes that have actions. Actions usually result in some form of commitment. For example, selecting the "OK" button in a software interface or pressing a button on a device results in a desired outcome. An operation is the outcome of the user's action. The operation is the program initiated and yields the results of the user's intended goal.

Journey Maps

Journey maps are a diagram that illustrates the steps your end-users go through in engaging with your company, services and software solution (Figure 4-3). Human behavior is driven by the innate need to satisfy identifiable as well as subconscious needs and goals. Journey maps help you connect your end-users' motivations to their behavior and how your solution meets their needs.

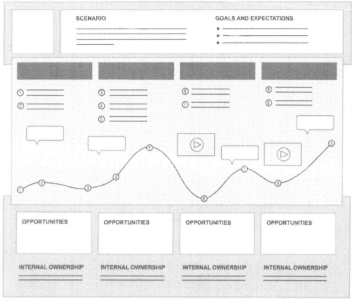

FIGURE 4-3: Journey map example

Journey maps help you to identify your end-users' barriers to your solutions and inform you how to improve the experience you deliver with your software. Develop journey maps to illustrate all the ways your end-users interact with your process and procedures that your end-users must follow to understand to achieve their goals. Take special note of the key interaction points – touch points – and what they like and dislike, what frustrates them or delights them. Getting these touch points right is the key for you to create experiences that meet your end-users' needs and create loyalty and advocacy for your software solutions and overall brand.

Iterative Design

User Experience Designers develop prototypes to conduct iterative reviews with customers to help defining the behavior of products and systems. When validating your new idea to the market, you may have to educate your customers so they can put your solution in a new context. This paradigm shift for the customer may not come easy and they may not understand the value of your new solution right away – especially if you cannot put it in context for them. Being able to put your new solution in context for your customers and users is the key to validating the solution meets their needs and is easy to use.

Low-Fidelity Prototypes

Develop low-fidelity prototypes like wireframes (Figure 4-4). Wireframes are a basic visual guide used to suggest the layout and placement of fundamental design elements in the interface. They provide a visual reference for the structure of the screens, define the positioning of global and secondary levels of the information hierarchy, and maintain design consistency throughout the application. Review these prototypes to ensure that the customers' and users' needs are understood. Validate that the general workflow navigation, information grouping, information hierarchy, terminology, labels and general interactions are correct. Do not be concerned with visual design at this point – in fact, the prototype should be void of all color, fonts, icons, graphics, etc. to keep the focus on the work flow and information design.

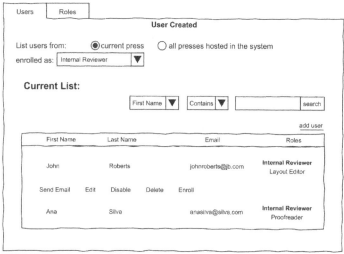

FIGURE 4-4: Low fidelity prototype example

When reviewing prototypes, validate where various customers' workflow and content overlap and differ and start thinking about the right design solution to support the differences in their workflow and content.

For web-based solutions, it can be as simple as leveraging login ID to drive customization – *if* company A *then* this screen, label, etc. *If* company B *then* this. If it's a desktop experience, then you may want to create an Admin area where each key customer can select the different options that fit their company's needs.

Involve Engineers as early as possible in the product lifecycle. When possible, share early research and design direction with the technology architects and engineers to ensure feasibility and technology innovation opportunities. The early prototypes are an excellent tool to work with Engineering on the best technical solution. Many times, the engineers know of future components or pieces of technology that can reduce or eliminate the need of a component or screen – enhancing the ease of use of the solution.

> For example, when developing the Add User wireframes for our User Management solution, the Engineers may know things

about the LDAP that may automate some steps in the process.

Medium-Fidelity Prototypes

Once you are confident that you understand your various customers' workflow and content then it is time to develop the visual design – color scheme, fonts, iconography, branding and all graphic elements. Work closely with the visual designer or visual design team to ensure that the visual design elements support the company's brand and enhance the ease of use of the application.

Develop medium-fidelity prototypes that reflect the information and visual design. Depending on how the design team is structured, this is a good time to bring in the interaction designers. Interaction Design defines the behavior of how your customers and users interact with your solution. Interaction design is focused on making products more useful, usable, and desirable.

Work with customers and users and conduct reviews of the prototypes for feedback. Wash, rinse and repeat as needed. This is an iterative, collaborative process that includes all the solution stakeholders.

High-Fidelity Prototypes

Depending on the organization's process and structure, high-fidelity prototypes may be developed (Figure 4-5). They may be the responsibility of UX Design or UI Development or a collaboration of both. High-fidelity prototypes accurately simulate user interactions. For web-based solutions, this includes development in mark-up languages like Hyper-Text Mark-up Language, Cascading Style Sheets, JavaScript, and user interface component libraries.

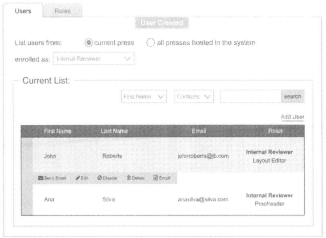

FIGURE 4-5: High fidelity prototype example

In some organizations, the high-fidelity prototypes are used for the presentation layer. If they are used for the final code then they need to be valid, compliant and follow the organization's coding standard.

Five Iterative Design Reviews in Five Days

A use research method that I like to use early in the product lifecycle is five iterative design reviews in five days. It goes like this:

Step One: Determine what the most important parts of your solution are in terms of your customers' success. Build a low-fidelity prototype that you can easily make changes to that represents these parts of your solution.

Step Two: Identify your target audiences. Profile your customers. For example, for your solution, your customers may use your software to make strategic decisions, tactical decisions or not modify it all and reap its benefits. Not modifying your solution at all may yield the best results while adjusting for tactical reasons may not have great long-term results but for your savvier clients, they may make small or brief adjustments to your software that yield better results for their specific business needs. You may categorize your customers in these group – strategic, tactical and happy campers. Work with your client representatives to help you profile your customers.

Step Three: Identify ideal clients to work with that represent each group. The clients that you choose need to have most of the qualities for the group they represent. You may need more than one client to represent all the qualities in the category. These clients need to be on good terms with your organization and be eager to help you make your software experience better.

Step Four: Recruit your clients for the user experience design review. Whoever owns the relationship with your client's needs to partner with you to contact the client, explain the design review goals, how it will benefit them and the logistics around how, when and where to participate.

Step Five: Run the iterative design reviews. You may conduct the design review as structured or unstructured as you want, as long as it's the best way to help you reach your goal, using qualitative or quantitative technique or a combination. You may run the review with precise questions for specific tasks that you want to evaluate or get general feedback on ease of use like the information architecture design. Focus on what your business determines is the most important for your customers' success.

Day one – meet with your first client. Review the design, ask a lot of questions, take good notes. That afternoon, make the changes to the prototype based on what you learned. There may be a lot of changes from the first review.

Day two – meet with your second client. Review the design, ask a lot of questions, take good notes. There may be things that you added from the first review that the second client will love and think that you are genius – this is innovation from listening to your customers. Enjoy it. That afternoon, make the changes to the prototype based on what you learned. Some of what you learned will validate what is working and rest will be tweaks.

Day Three through Five – same routine – review, learn, make changes. You will see your design become more solid with each review. It will become clear what is easy to use and you gain great insight into what your customers see as innovated. They will think that you are a genius by the end of day five.

In a Nutshell

✓ UX research and high-level design help determine the investment themes, vision, architecture and feature set through research and high-level design activities.

✓ User stories communicate the software requirements in a simple sentence in the language of the end-user that capture their goals.

✓ A Minimal Viable Product (MVP) is a product with just enough features to gather validated learning about the product and its continued development while a Minimum Desirable Product (MDP) focuses primarily on whether you are providing a great product experience that creates value for your customers.

✓ In most cases, your customers and users don't know what they want... The best solutions are usually something that customers and the users have never thought of. The real value that the software solution provider brings is the ability to deliver a solution that is better than they could imagine through user research

CHAPTER 5

Usability: Making Sure You Got It Right

"Any darn fool can make something complex; it takes a genius to make something simple."

— *Albert Einstein*

Later in the product lifecycle, the User Experience Designer provides cross-component and cross-program design guidance to provide a consistent user experience across the components and systems of the larger solution. Now in the process, feature sets are broken down into releases. UX detailed designs are reviewed with customers and evaluated with end-users to determine the final UX design for this release of the software.

Usability Evaluations

Once you have validated that the workflow meets the customer and user needs then you should evaluate the tasks to ensure that they are easy to complete. Usability evaluations assess the degree to which the system can be operated by its users, the efficiency of the solution and satisfaction. These evaluations are to validate that the tasks are easy to complete – it is a test of the ease of use of the application, not the intelligence of the users. If the tasks are hard or impossible to complete, then the system is not easy to use.

For example, for the User Management solution's Add User, you will want to provide a scenario for the evaluation: "You need to add a new employee to the system." Then you will observe the participant to see if they can complete the task. Do they need assistance to complete the task or is it obvious what they need to do to add a user?

Usability Specialists conduct usability evaluations with end-user to ensure that the tasks are not only effective and efficient but also delightful. They work with customers and users to conduct reviews of prototypes for feedback. The metrics for effectiveness, efficiency and delight are task completion, task time and emotional response. There are several types of evaluation methods that may be used:

Internal Evaluations

Internal evaluations may be held with stakeholders, subject matter experts, and/or end-user proxies to validate that the design meets the clients' needs. This is a fast and easy way to ensure that you are on the right track. It is a recommended step before reviewing with real clients.

Remote Moderated Evaluations

Remote evaluations are an easy and inexpensive way to evaluate designs. You may conduct remote evaluations with internal stakeholders and/or external clients. Remote evaluations give you more flexibility in scheduling evaluations with people across great distances. It is easy to record the session with most standard conferencing systems. What you lose in remote evaluations are the subtle facial queues and body language and the intimacy and trust of spending time with your client.

Remote Unmoderated Evaluations

UX professionals can run unmoderated, task-based studies with geographically dispersed participants over any web-based interface (website, prototype, mock-up). Participants take the study simultaneously (asynchronous), in their natural context, using their own PC or device. Unlike traditional in-lab user testing, remote unmoderated testing does not require a moderator or lab facilities and enables you to reduce costs, save time, recruit with ease and improve the frequency of usability testing.

Lab Evaluations

Formal evaluations may be held in a usability lab. This may be a third-party lab that hosts the evaluations for your organization or your organization may have its own lab. The advantage of a lab is the ability to control almost all aspects of evaluations – lighting, sound, interruptions, etc. Others associated with the product may observe the evaluations from behind a two-way mirror or monitor. Having the people involved with determining, developing and deploying the solution observing actual people interacting with it is always an eye opener. The disadvantage of a lab setting compared to a site visit is that you don't get the full context of your solution in the environment where it will be used.

Site Visit Evaluations

Evaluating your solution at your clients' place of use requires more logistical coordination, travel time and related cost. But evaluating your solution in the setting where it is being used is the best way to understand its context of use. You will observe the various lighting, sounds, distractions, cheat sheets, workarounds, etc., giving you a wealth of knowledge how your system is really being used and a ton of ideas for innovations.

You may do some or all or none of these methods depending on your budget, time, resources and other factors. I highly recommend that you find some way to evaluate whether your solution is easy to use – even if it means grabbing some people from a hallway and getting them to try to complete the basic tasks. One usability evaluation is better than none. A couple is better than one and several is better than a couple. Studies have shown that conducting five usability evaluations with your target end-user will find 85% of your usability issues. The earlier in the product lifecycle you can evaluate your solution, the earlier you may correct your usability issues – the more money you save in development and the more revenue you gain with adoption, retention and advocacy. In today's enterprise software market, applications need to be easy to use. Good technology is ubiquitous or invisible. Customers and users have come to expect easy-to-use solutions. In today's mature software market where the technological solutions are similar, usability is an important differentiator when considering a purchase as important as an enterprise solution.

Accessibility

Accessibility is a general term used to describe the degree to which a product, device, service or environment is available to as many people as possible. Accessibility can be viewed as the "ability to access" the promised possible benefit of some system or entity. Accessibility is often focused on people with disabilities or special needs and their right of access to entities, often through use of assistive technology.

Accessibility testing is a subset of usability testing wherein the users under consideration are people with all abilities and disabilities. The significance of this testing is to verify both usability and accessibility. Accessibility aims to cater people of different abilities such as:

- Visual Impairment
- Physical Impairment
- Hearing Impairment
- Cognitive Impairment
- Learning Impairment

A good software solution should cater to all sets of people and NOT be limited just to disabled people. These include:

- Users with poor communications infrastructure
- Older people and new users, who are often computer illiterate
- Users using old system (NOT capable of running the latest software)
- Users who are using NON-Standard Equipment
- Users who are having restricted access

There are software tools to assist with conformance evaluations. These tools range from specific issues such as color blindness to tools that will perform automated testing.

Apple includes assistive technology in its products as standard features. For example, iPhone, iPad, iPod, and Mac OS X include screen magnification and VoiceOver, a screen-access technology, for the blind and visually impaired. To assist those with cognitive and learning disabilities, every Mac includes an alternative, simplified user interface that rewards exploration and learning. And, for those who find it difficult to use a mouse, every Mac computer includes Mouse Keys, Slow Keys and Sticky Keys, which adapt the computer to the user's needs and capabilities.

Pre-Development Usability Evaluations

The rule of thumb in many usability-aware organizations is that the cost-benefit ratio for usability is $1:$10-$100. Once a system is in development, correcting a problem costs 10 times as much as fixing the same problem in design. If the system has been released, it costs 100 times as much relative to fixing in design (Gilb 1988). Eighty-five percent of the issues can be identified by evaluating the system with as few as three iterations with five users (Nielsen & Landauer, 1993).

Conduct the evaluations on workflows and tasks that the customers and users determined to be most critical. Measure the efficiency, effectiveness and satisfaction by time on task; completion of task; and expected and actual perceived easiness of task. Seventy percent completion of tasks for first-time users with little or no instruction is considered a pass rate by most software producers.

Correct any issues in the design from iteration to iteration. Document the evaluations in reports that explain who participated in the evaluations, what was evaluated, how it was measured, the findings and recommendations based on the findings. Use these findings and recommendations to determine the final design and develop design specifications for Development.

Post Release Usability Evaluations

After your software has been in production for six to eight weeks, conduct a follow-up usability evaluation to ensure that all the issues have been addressed properly and measure your usability ROI. For example, if you know the number of service calls associated with a specific task in the previous release, measure it now and compare with the new release. Multiply the number of calls reduced by the cost of a call and that is the actual dollars saved by this design. Document your ROI and any other issues that may have been discovered that you can incorporate in your next release.

Look at your analytics for insights. Look at where your users are clicking. Click tracking and heat maps reveal where your users are spending their time. If they are not clicking on the right elements then you have something you need to fix.

You may also look at what your users are entering in your Search. This will give you an idea of what you need to make clearer for them. Things they are looking often reveal what is not obvious to them. The keywords that they use are clues about where you need to improve your information design and experience.

Just like with pre-development usability evaluations, post-release evaluations may be in a usability lab onsite, at a neutral location, remotely with a web conference, unmoderated remotely with a third-party vendor or going to your customer where they use your solution.

Validate Key Interface Elements with Target Clients through Sales in 24 hours

We were designing a new interface for a new market. We were moving fast and needed to finalize our requirements for development in the next two days. There was one screen that we identified as key to the success of our end-users (the "money screen") and we wanted to validate that we got it was right – or what to change – before we finalized our requirement. We had a UX advocate in Sales who could share this with some key clients, get their feedback and get it back to us in the 24 hours. We did it with a screenshot and email.

We got the feedback, made some tweaks and got the updated requirements to development for the iteration in time. The new product went out and the customers thought it was "intuitive." We made it easy to use.

The lesson here is that you can validate ease of use fast.

Step 1: Ensure you know who your target audience is and what their goals are.
Step 2: Know the user interaction element or elements in your interface that are key to your target audience achieving their goal. It is usually one screen – the "money screen"
Step 3: Review the interface with your target and evaluate it against their goal for success
Step 4: Pay attention, take good notes and make the changes necessary for their success

It is that simple.

In a Nutshell

✓ Usability evaluations validate that the tasks are easy to complete – it is a test of the ease of use of the application, not the intelligence of the users. If the tasks are hard or impossible to complete, then the system is not easy to use.

✓ The metrics for effectiveness, efficiency and delight are task completion, task time and emotional response.

✓ Find some way to evaluate whether your solution is easy to use – even if it means grabbing some people from a hallway and getting them to try to complete the basic tasks. One usability evaluation is better than none.

✓ The earlier in the product lifecycle you evaluate your solution, the earlier you may correct your usability issues, the more money you save in development and the more revenue you gain with adoption, retention and advocacy.

✓ Conduct a follow-up usability evaluation after a release to ensure that all the issues have been addressed properly and measure your usability ROI.

CHAPTER 6

User Experience in Development

"Design is not just what it looks like and feels like. Design is how it works."

— Steve Jobs

Design Sprints take the five stages of Design Thinking (Empathize, Define, Ideate, Prototype, and Test) and do them in five days (Figure 6-1). Design Sprints are perfect for solving an important issue that is small enough to digest in five days.

In the larger cycle of Idea, Build, Launch and Learn, Design Sprint does a quick Idea-Learn loop prior to Build for better releases. The idea is that working together in a design sprint, you can shortcut the endless-debate cycle and compress months of time into a single week. Instead of waiting to launch a MVP to understand if an idea is any good, you'll get clear data from a realistic prototype. The sprint gives you a superpower: You can fast-forward into the future to see your finished product and customer reactions, before making any expensive commitments.

Start with putting together a multi-disciplinary team based on the problem that needs to be solved. This may include a Product Owner, Engineer, UX Researcher and Designer and other subject matter experts that understand the market, business or customer needs. It is revolutionary to see non-designers express their ideas and evolutionary for the organizations to get everyone involved in Design Thinking.

FIGURE 6-1: Design sprints day 1-5 example

Day One – understand the problem you are trying to solve and get everyone on the same page. Having a good facilitator can make or break the whole process. Ask yourselves, "Who are our users and what are their needs?" Put yourselves in your customer's shoes. What is the context in which they are using your solution? How do your competitors solve this problem? What do the reviewers say about your solution? Ask the right question and formulate a strategy.

Day Two – diverge down many paths and explore ideas. Envision what is possible. Brainstorm as many possibilities that you can. Get everyone involved and sketch possible solutions.

Day Three – determine the final design to test, the "hypothesis" or "experiment." Choose the best idea and create a rough storyboard of how you envision it working to inform the prototype design.

Day Four – build out the high-level prototype for testing. This should be an iterative process, too, that involves all the key stakeholders all along the way. Build something quickly. It doesn't have to be perfect – just enough to test your idea.

Day Five – test your prototype with real live target customers! Get the right people in your test that match the persona that you decided on during Day One. Run your test script and prototype before testing it with your target to ensure that the test questions all make sense and that the prototype works the way it needs to.

Design sprints are intense! They are a week of 6-7 hour days. You are constantly working, evaluating, sketching, discussing, voting, testing. You do a tremendous amount of work in a single week.

The test results may reveal that it is feasible – you can make it – but not viable – your target audience doesn't want it. This is good to know early in your product lifecycle so you don't waste time and resources defining, developing and delivering something your customers don't want. You may realize that it is a great idea but belongs in another solution in your portfolio or that it is much bigger effort – more than just a feature. It may be a whole new module. And that is exactly why we do Design Sprints!

User Experience Collaboration with Development

Most solutions' elements interact with the user in some fashion, so proper UX design is as important (or sometimes even more important) than other aspects of good software system engineering, especially in larger systems. This impacts that the way in which UX Designers collaborate with the rest of the program. The following two organizational models are the most common.

Centralized UX Guidance and Implementation

Although it might appear attractive from the perspective of empowerment and velocity of the agile team, fully distributing UX development to the team can be quite problematic. Therefore, some organizations create a central user experience design team that iterates somewhat independently from the development teams. They run a common cadence and iteration model, but their backlog will contain user experience story spikes, user experience testing, prototyping and implementation activities that are used to determine a common user experience. They typically work one or two iterations ahead to discover upcoming functionality and determine how it should be implemented.

It is important to note that the purpose of the centralized UX team is to maintain a consistent user experience across the enterprise solution's entire product portfolio. For this to be successful, UX resources must be integrated into the product teams to best meet the individual product's specific market, customer and end-user needs. Each product has unique needs that a dedicated UX Lead must have a deep understanding of to design the experience in context of these target customers and end-users while being mindful of the general UX standard guidelines across the portfolio. The UX product team lead must think "globally" in terms of the portfolio standards and guidelines but design solutions "locally" for the product that they serve.

Distributed, Governed UX Development

In the case where a central team becomes a bottleneck for the development teams, a distributed but governed UX development may be best. In the "distributed but governed" model, there is a small, centralized UX design team who provides the basic design standards and preliminary mock-ups for each UI, but the teams have team-based UX implementation experts for the implementation. In this case, the UX experts are distributed among the teams, but the centralized authority provides HTML designs, CSS style sheets, brand control, mock-ups, usability guidelines and other artifacts that provide conceptual integrity of the UX across the entire solution. The central team also typically attends iteration and PSI/release demos to see how the overall system design is progressing.

Each model has its merits and it is up to each organization to determine what best meets their needs. As with all things, trial and error will evolve the organization structure, disciplines and collaboration.

UX Debt

The term "UX debt" comes to us from the term "Technical Debt" coined by Ward Cunningham (Cunningham). Technical debt (sometimes called code debt) is "a concept in programming that reflects the extra development work that arises when code that is easy to implement in the short run is used instead of applying the best overall solution" according to Cunningham. Basically, this means there are costs of cleaning up less-than-ideal code. It is "debt" because you need "pay it off" – go back and rewrite the less-than-ideal code. If you don't, then there can be less-than-ideal consequences that can affect your customers' experience – sending them to your competition.

Joshua Kerievsky is credited with extended the technical debt metaphor to user experience design using the term "User Experience (UX) Debt" (Dunwoody & Rector, 2015). Kerievsky explained that, like technical debt, UX debt will eventually come due, usually in the form of less customer satisfaction and possible customer defects. Just like technical debt, UX debt must also be addressed.

Fixing your UX Debt is a relatively straightforward endeavor. Jack Moffett shares this 3-Step Guide to Erasing Your UX Debt (Moffett):

Step 1: Create and Validate a UX Debt Inventory. Review your support call logs, analytics data, customer surveys and interview results and make a list of your top UX issues.

Step 2: Prioritization. Rank your issue issues by severity. This could be a usability severity rating based on task completion or time on task or customer satisfaction score or based on the number of support calls or lost revenue due to the issues. Create a scorecard based on these factors and/or others, whatever is most important to your organization.

You can create a matrix of severity of issues over estimated time to fix to determine the order that issues get fixed.

Step 3: Schedule. Your debt doesn't get paid off until you fix it. You need to have the discipline to build "debt payment" into your development schedule. This will require that the decision makers in your organization understand the cost of the debt and a clearly articulated plan to address it.

Though the UX team may be accountable for identifying, defining and prioritizing the UX debt, it takes Development to ensure that the UX debt gets addressed. You may address this in periodic dedicated iterations or address one or two UX debt issues in every iteration. It is up to the organization to determine what makes the most sense for themselves based on their business strategy. Of course, the best way to limit UX debt is to design it right in the first place.

Organizing Your UX Team for Success

Over the years, I have developed and enhanced several UX teams. In some cases, I had to start with a pre-existing dysfunctional team and in other cases, I got to start from scratch. Starting from scratch is easier.

When starting an experience design team from a blank slate, start with understanding the market problem that your organization is solving and your organization's overall vision, mission and strategy. Based on these, determine your experience design vision, mission and strategy to align with the organization. From there, you can determine the processes you need to integrate, the talent that you need to hire and a growth path that aligns with your organization's experience design needs.

In most cases, start by bringing in an Interaction Designer to build prototypes. Start developing low, medium and high prototypes for early, mid and late product lifecycle. Everyone will see the immediate value of prototyping. A picture is worth a thousand words and a prototype is worth a thousand meetings. Prototypes accelerate clarity.

Next, introduce usability. Now that you have prototypes, you can test them with internal subject matter experts and actual customers and end-users. This feedback will move you from educated guesses to what your customers want to data-driven new insights.

As your experience design organization matures, introduce user research. User research is a main driver in innovation. It will get you out and ahead of your marketplace and may even bring you into new markets. But user research needs prototyping and testing to vet concepts and validate ideas.

If you are starting with an existing dysfunctional team, then you need to do the proper analysis to determine what is working and your opportunities for improvement. It is a similar process to developing your strategy scorecard with a focus on organization and operation refinement.

In a Nutshell

✓ UX designs, guidelines and specifications need to be completed prior to the target development iteration so developers and tester can focus on developing and testing the working software.

✓ Some organizations have a central user experience design team that iterates somewhat independently from the development teams while other organizations have a distributed but governed model where a small, centralized UX design team provides the basic design standards.

✓ UX debt will eventually come due, usually in the form of less customer satisfaction and possible customer defects. Just like technical debt, UX debt must also be addressed.

✓ Instead of waiting for launch to understand if an idea is any good, try a quick prototype in a Design Sprint.

CHAPTER 7

Building Your User Organization

"Individuals and Interactions Over Processes and Tools."

– Manifesto for Agile Software Development

The Manifesto for Agile Software Development states that individuals and interactions are more important than processes and tools. This means that individuals and interactions are more important to successfully develop software than the process they follow or the tools that they use. You may have the best processes and tools in the world but it is the individuals and their interaction that make it successful. Having an effective, efficient process that is clearly understood and the right tools to do your job is still necessary but means nothing without effective individual interactions to define, design, develop and deliver your software.

The main purpose of the UX team is to maintain a consistent user experience across the enterprise solution's entire product portfolio. For this to be successful, UX resources must be integrated into the product teams to best meet the individual product's specific market, customer and end-user needs. Each product has unique needs that a dedicated UX Lead must have a deep understanding of to design the experience in context of these target customers and end-users while being mindful of the general UX standard guidelines across the portfolio. The UX product team lead must think "globally" in terms of the portfolio standards and guidelines but design solutions "locally" for the product that they serve.

Understand Your Vision and Strategy

What is your organization's vision and strategy and how does the experience you deliver to your customers support it? Your vision is probably to be the industry leader for your market. And your strategy is to be better and different then your competition. So how are you better and different than your competitors? Describe what that means for your customers, and then you can articulate your user experience strategy in context of your organization's overall objectives.

Your market and customers have a specific need for which you provide a solution. Markets are made up of segments and segments are made up of customers and customers can be described by their motivations, needs and goals and how you help them achieve them.

For example, let's say you are an online service provider. You provide a subscription-based service that is easy to use for your customers. How do you know it is "easy to use" to your customer? Not what *you* think is easy to use but what *your customers* think is easy to use. That is your UX strategy.

User Experience KPI

Based on your organization's overall objectives, what are your UX objectives? What are your measures for success? What are your Key Performance Indicators (KPI)? You need to be clear on how you measure your user experience objectives in context of the overall success of your organization. What is your metric?

For example, you may want to increase customer conversion – the number of prospective customers that visit your website to purchase your solution. Conversion is a KPI. You may set a goal for a 20% increase of new visitors to make a purchase. You may measure that by how many new visitors click the "buy" button. That sounds easy enough but it will be your user experience design that will attract them and guide them to this conclusion.

Organization's Process and UX Fit

Your organization has processes now. They may not be well defined or understood – or even consistent – but somehow you are getting things done. You need to understand your own process well enough to determine where your user experience development fits.

For example, you may have a great solution for your market but the experience you are delivering is not getting the customers you were hoping. Where are you defining, developing and delivering your experience in your process? Not surprising, the earlier you address this issue in your process, the bigger your return on investment in downstream processes.

The Talent that Makes It Happen

There are many disciplines that fall under the umbrella of User Experience. In general, someone with the title "UX Researcher" or "Usability Engineer" will have a background in research and human behavior. They may have a degree in Anthropology or Ethnology. They are skilled at conducting research, developing usability plans, conducting studies, analyzing data, determining findings and providing recommendations. In larger organizations, "Research" and "Usability" may be separate roles.

If you have a lot of content or data, you may have a "Content Manager" or an "information Architect." They may have a background in Writing or Library Science. They are skilled at managing content and information design: terminology, titles, labels, logical grouping of content, information hierarchy and data visualization.

A "Visual Designer" or "Graphic Designer" may have a background in Communication or Graphic Design. They understand color, typography, layout and illustration. They develop color schemes, visual design comps, graphics, illustrations, icons and style guides.

An "Interaction Designer" may have a background in Human-Computer Interaction (HCI) or Cognitive Science. They understand human behavior, metaphors and design patterns. They are skilled at developing prototypes. They understand design principles and industry best practices like when to use radio buttons instead of a drop-down menu or when to use tabs, and swipe and tap behaviors.

If you are making hardware or devices then you will need an "Industrial Designer." If you do a lot of animation or Virtual Reality, you may have an "Animator" or "Motion Graphics Artist." If you are designing wearables then you may need a "Textile Designer."

Ask yourself, "What UX activities are needed for our process?" That determines the needed skills and who you need to hire. Is your solution considered hard to use by your customers? Is it hard for your customers to understand your value to them? Are your customers even finding you? Based on how you answer these questions determine what type of UX talent you need.

For example, let's say you are getting plenty of customers visiting your website but have a high abandonment of your purchase process. I would recommend hiring UX experts who can help redesign your purchasing experience. This could be an interaction designer to prototype a better experience or a visual designer to develop a cleaner, more cohesive look and feel or a usability specialist that could do a little UX research, develop and execute a usability study and provide findings and recommendations. It may take all these skills in some degree depending on your specific situation.

Having a clear understanding of how your UX strategy fits in your company's overall vision will guide you on your UX KPIs, where it fits in your overall process and determine the talent that you need to hire to deliver an experience that will win the hearts of your customers.

Hiring the Right Skills for the Right Job

It is not uncommon for me to find an organization that has had a bad User Experience experience. Leaders in the organizations know that UX is important and they hire people that they feel are right for the job. If the person hiring the UX talent is not a UX expert themselves then there is a good chance that they may hire the wrong fit.

In one organization that I worked with, they needed a usability specialist to test their software interface interaction. The person hiring the usability specialist was not an UX expert and hired a graphic designer who had a lot of user experience and usability references on their resume. To be fair, the Graphic Designer probably thought they knew usability well enough to test enterprise software (how different could it be from the websites that they designed?).

As you may have guessed, the website Graphic Designer didn't understand the task-based application software enough to develop and run usability evaluations.

Their next hire was a Human Factors Engineer. Though this sounds promising, the HFE had spent their entire career with human-machine interaction (HMI) testing plane cockpit controls. That did not translate well to human-computer interactions of software. This didn't work either.

This organizations brought in a UX expert to hire a UX specialist. The UX expert found a usability specialist with experience testing enterprise software. This specialist had many years of experience testing tasked-based software application experiences. They knew what to look for, how to design the right test, recruit the right evaluators, run the test and report the finding and recommendations to improve the usability of the software interface.

Another organization that wanted to start a UX group hired a UX Manager in QA. Again, the leader knew they needed to improve the user experience of their software and knew that they needed to hire someone with skills in usability testing for enterprise software. The problem was the UX leader was only a Manager and in QA. Because they were QA, they would run studies of finished product and report on changes that they would have to make in the next release (you can guess how that went over…) and since they were only a manager in QA, no one listened to them. The whole thing crashed and burned within months.

The organization hired a UX Director in Architecture. From Architecture, the UX leader got a holistic perspective of the software solution and could see the future direction of the business. From there, the UX leader developed the business's UX strategy and hired the right people to execute the strategy.

To hire the right UX talent, you need a UX expert that has a deep understand of your technology and business needs.

In a Nutshell

✓ Having an effective, efficient process that is clearly understood and the right tools to do your job is necessary but means nothing without effective individual interactions to define, design, develop and deliver your software.

✓ Each product has unique needs that a dedicated UX Lead must have a deep understanding of in order to design the experience in context of these target customers and end-users while being mindful of the general UX standard guidelines across the portfolio.

✓ The UX product team lead must think "globally" in terms of the portfolio standards and guidelines but design solutions "locally" for the product that they serve.

✓ Understand Your Vision, Strategy and KPIs.

✓ Understand your organization's process and UX Fit

Bibliography

Apple. http://developer.apple.com/ue/.
In-text reference: (Apple)

Brown, Tim., *Change by Design.* New York: Harper,
2009.
In-text reference: (Brown, 2009)

Charan, Ram. *What the CEO Wants You to Know.* United
States: Crown Business, 2001.
In-text reference: (Charan, 2001)

Cunningham, Ward. *Ward Explains Debt Metaphor.*
http://wiki.c2.com/?WardExplainsDebtMetaphor
In-text reference: (Cunningham)

Gilb, Tom. *Principles of Software Engineering Management.*
Boston: Addison-Wesley, 1988.
In-text reference: (Gilb, 1988)

Dunwoody, Kimberly and Susan Teague Rector. "UX
Debt in the Enterprise: A Practical Approach" *User
Experience Magazine*, 15(1). 2015.
In-text reference: (Dunwoody & Rector, 2015)

Moffett, Jack. *The 3-Step Guide to Erasing Your UX Debt*,
https://www.uxpin.com/studio/blog/3-step-guide-
erasing-ux-debt/
In-text reference: (Moffett)

Nielsen, Jakob and Donald Norman. *The Definition of*

User Experience (UX),
https://www.nngroup.com/articles/definition-user-experience/
In-text reference: (Nielsen & Norman)

Nielsen, Jakob, and Thomas K. Landauer. "A mathematical model of the finding of usability problems," *Proceedings of ACM INTERCHI'93 Conference.* Amsterdam, The Netherlands, 24-29 April 1993.
In-text reference: (Nielsen & Landauer, 1993)

Norman, Donald. "Human-Centered Design Considered Harmful." *Interactions*, July + August, 2005.

Norman, Donald. *The Design of Everyday Things.* New York: Basic Books, 2002.
In-text reference: (Norman, 2002)

Pine II, B. Joseph and James H. Gilmore. *Welcome to the Experience Economy. Harvard Business Review.* 1998
In-text reference: (Pine & Gilmore, 1998)

Pine II, B. Joseph and James H. Gilmore. *The Experience Economy: Work Is Theater & Every Business is a Stage.* Boston: Harvard Business Press, 1999.
In-text reference: (Pine & Gilmore, 1999)

Van Tyne, Sean (contributing writer). *The Guide to the Product Management and Marketing Body of Knowledge.* Association of International Product Marketing & Management. 2013.

Van Tyne, Sean and Bean, Jeofrey. *The Customer Experience Revolution: How Companies like Apple, Amazon,*

and Starbucks Have Changed Business Forever. St. Johnsbury, VT: Brigantine Media, 2012.
In-text reference: (Bean & Van Tyne, 2012)

Van Tyne, Sean. "Corporate UX Maturity: A Model for Organizations." *UX Magazine*, Volume 9, Issue 1, 2010.

Van Tyne, Sean. "Defining and Designing Technology for People." *Pragmatic Marketing*, Volume 8, Issue 2, 2010.

Van Tyne, Sean. *Corporate User-Experience Maturity Model. Human Centered Design.* Springer Berlin / Heidelberg, 2009, Volume 5619/2009, pages 635-639. ISBN: 978-3-642-02805-2

Van Tyne, Sean. "Product Design: Bridging the Gap Between Product Management and Development." *The Pragmatic Marketer*, Volume 5, Issue 1, 2007

Van Tyne, Sean. "Easy to Use for Whom: Defining the Customer and User Experience for Enterprise Software." *The Pragmatic Marketer*, Volume 5, Issue 3, 2007

About the Author

Sean Van Tyne is the author of *Easy to Use: User Experience Design in Agile Development for Enterprise Software,* co-author of *The Customer Experience Revolution: How Companies Like Apple, Amazon, and Starbucks Have Changed Business Forever,* and a contributing author for *The Guide to the Product Management and Marketing Body of Knowledge (the ProdBOK® Guide).*

International speaker, best-selling author and advisor, Sean is an industry leader who helps organizations with their strategies, goals and direction to deliver innovative solutions with best-in-class experiences to increase customer satisfaction, loyalty and advocacy that creates sustainable long-term revenue.

43349024R00077

Made in the USA
Middletown, DE
07 May 2017